BOOK 1

BIRDS OF THE LOCALITY

BOOK 2

HISTORY, MYTH & LEGEND

BOOK 3

A GUIDE OF THE LOCALITY

BOOK 4

CORNELIUS O'BRIEN M.P.

The Cliffs of Moher Visitor Experience

Millions of visitors have enjoyed the richness of the Cliffs of Moher over the centuries. Its wild beauty and majesty, its unsurpassed vistas, its teeming wildlife and dizzying heights beckon to people from across Ireland and across the world. I am delighted that my brother, Matthew, has decided to republish these four guide booklets as a single volume. We hope that the insights and information herein will enrich your visit to one of Ireland's and the world's true natural treasures.

Eamonn Kelly | Author

In February 2007, the Cliffs of Moher Visitor Experience opened to the public: An award-winning, eco-friendly underground building that houses restaurants, gift shop, tourist information, a first aid room and an exciting new exhibition, entitled Atlantic Edge. The new facilities include a craftworkers street of six shops, picnic areas and restoration work at O'Brien's Tower. In addition to the new Visitor Centre, improvements and extension have been made to the cliff edge pathways, steps and the viewing area. A new visitor management programme was also introduced that involves Cliffs of Moher Rangers who offer the public information on the cliffs, guided tours and conservation measures. The work begun in the nineteenth century by Cornelius O'Brien to welcome visitors from near and far to the Cliffs of Moher continues in this state-of-the-art development.

Katherine Webster | Cliffs of Moher Visitor Experience

BOOK 1

THE CLIFFS OF MOHER

BIRDS OF THE LOCALITY

EAMONN KELLY B.Ed., Ph.D.

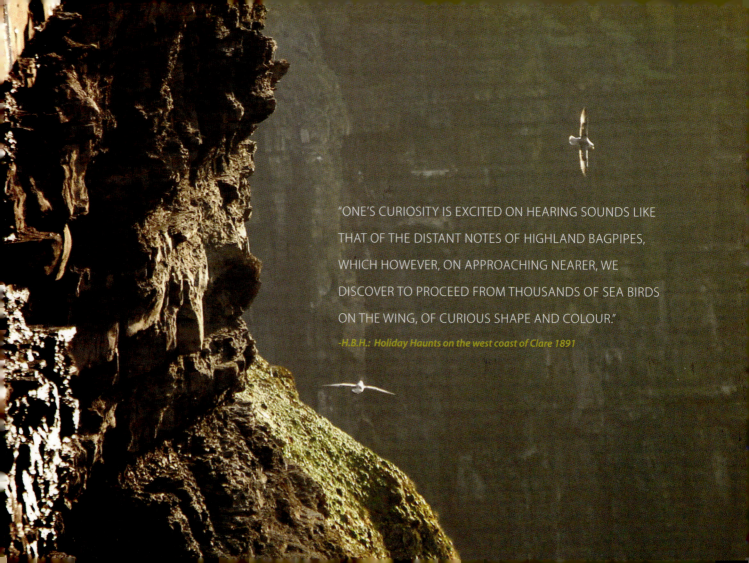

"ONE'S CURIOSITY IS EXCITED ON HEARING SOUNDS LIKE THAT OF THE DISTANT NOTES OF HIGHLAND BAGPIPES, WHICH HOWEVER, ON APPROACHING NEARER, WE DISCOVER TO PROCEED FROM THOUSANDS OF SEA BIRDS ON THE WING, OF CURIOUS SHAPE AND COLOUR."

-H.B.H.: *Holiday Haunts on the west coast of Clare 1891*

Images clockwise from top left
Gannet,
Guillemot,
Fulmar,
Kittiwake

A rich variety of birdlife is to be found in and around the Cliffs of Moher. For the naturalist, the area is a constant delight. The following are examples of some of the area's birds.

Breanan Mór Sea Stack:
Fulmar's wheeling on the updrafts

Facing Page:
Fulmar's nesting area

Razorbills

Cormorant

The Cormorant is noted for its voracious appetite eating up to its own weight in fish daily. This sea bird surprisingly does not have waterproofing oil on its feathers; as a consequence it can often be seen standing on large rocks drying its wings. The Cormorant, with its close relative the Shag, can be seen on Carrig a dTrial at the tip of Aill na Shearrach – See Ordnance Map, Page 38 - also on the base of An Branán Mór Sea Stack beneath O'Brien's Tower.

Cormorant

SHAG

Being related to the Cormorant, the Shag can be distinguished by the lack of the white face patch. Its breeding grounds are similar to those of the Cormorant.

Shag

Shags nesting

BOOK I · BIRDS OF THE LOCALITY | 11

CHOUGH

A land bird of the crow family that is now becoming rare in Europe. Its main holding is on the West Coast of Ireland. Distinguishing features are: red curved beak, red legs, and an undulating flight (length: 40 cm, wingspan: 82 cm, weight: M/F: 310 g). The Chough has a loud "che-oww" call.

RAVEN

Also of the crow family and again quite rare. Thirteen pairs were counted on the Cliffs in 1974. The Raven is the biggest crow (length: 64 cm, wingspan: 135 cm, weight: M: 1.3 kg   F: 1.1 kg). Ravens are easy birds to distinguish, being very large and rolling occasionally on their backs as they fly. Ravens have a low hoarse call.

Raven

FLIGHT PATTERN OF THE RAVEN

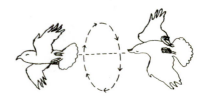

Chough

GREAT BLACK BACKED/ LESSER BLACK BACKED GULL

These related birds are among the largest Irish sea gulls. The Great Black Backed (length: 71 cm, wingspan: 158 cm, weight: M/F: 1.7 kg). It is larger than the Lesser Black Backed gull and has red feet as opposed to yellow of the Lesser Black Backed (length: 58 cm, wingspan: 142 cm, weight: M/F: 830 g). Both can be found along most of the cliff face.

FLIGHT PATTERN OF THE CHOUGH

Great Black Backed Gull

GANNET

This large sea bird is unmistakable (length: 94 cm, wingspan: 172 cm, weight: M/F: 3 kg). It fishes by diving to the sea from heights up to 30.48 m above the waves. The Gannet is not resident on the Cliffs of Moher, but is a frequent visitor to the area. Small Skellig, a small island in the Atlantic Ocean some 12 km southwest of Valentia Island, County Kerry, is home to 27,000 pairs of Gannets, the second largest colony in the world.

PUFFIN

Sometimes called the "sea parrot", this bird is the most colourful on the Cliffs and distinguished by its highly attractive beak (length: 28 cm, wingspan: 55 cm, weight: M/F: 400 g). Goat Island (i.e. the promontory visible in the photograph on the right) is their major stronghold where they live in burrows in the green banks. Another colony exists beneath O'Brien's Tower facing towards Aill na Shearrach. Further colonies can be seen on green patches on the Cliff south of the viewing platform.

RAZORBILL

This bird is related to the Puffin, but does not have as colourful a bill. Like Guillemots, they can be found in much the same areas as Cormorants.

Facing Page: **The historic photograph on the right from the Lawrence Collection shows O'Brien's Tower in its original form 1835. Visible on the left is Goat Island where many of these seabirds may be found.**

GUILLEMOT

The Guillemot (Length: 40 cm, wingspan: 67 cm, weight: M/F: 690 g), while very similar to the Razorbill (length: 38 cm, wingspan: 66 cm, weight: M/F: 710 g), can be distinguished by its browner plumage and pointed beak.

KITTIWAKE

The Kittiwake (length: 39 cm, wingspan: 108 cm, weight: M/F: 410 g) is said to take its name from its cry; this bird has always been associated with the Cliffs. Its plaintive cry is said to echo the screams of those starving people who fell to their deaths seeking seabird eggs as food during the Great Famine (1845 - 1848). Large numbers of these birds can be seen on the cliff face south of the viewing platform.

PEREGRINE FALCON

The Peregrine (length: 42 cm, wingspan: 102 cm, weight: M: 670 g F: 1.1 kg) is the rarest bird on the cliffs. Only one pair of birds was recorded there in 1974. Two pairs were recorded in 2005. There were at least 2 pairs in 2008. These magnificent birds are noted for their terrific dives on prey, reaching speeds up to 332 km when diving.

FULMAR

The Fulmar (length: 48 cm, wingspan: 107 cm, weight: M: 880 g F: 730 g) is a cream-coloured bird, whose distinguishing mark is its large tubular nostrils. This bird is present all along the cliffs, wheeling on the updraughts from the Atlantic.

Fulmar

Herring Gull

HERRING GULL

This bird (length: 60 cm, wingspan: 144 cm, weight: M: 1.2 kg   F: 948) is common on the Cliffs and is a scavenger. Large flocks are often seen flying in the wake of trawlers. This gull, with the black headed gull, is the most frequent inland traveller.

An Branán Mór Sea Stack – a towering fortress for the Gulls and Choughs

OTHER BIRDS

Other birds that can be seen in the general area of Lahinch are: Herons – on the marsh between Liscannor and Lahinch. Rooks – there is a large rookery beside the first farm house one meets on the road from the Cliffs to Liscannor. Wheatears, Flycatchers and Pipits can be seen on the grass walls along the cliff paths. The rarest bird that has been recorded as being seen in the area is the Twite, which is a member of the finch family and has a Red status for protection (the highest).

Jackdaws are common all over the area as are Sparrows, Robins, Blackbirds, Magpies, Starlings, Hooded Crows, Skylarks, and – in season – Swifts, Swallows and Sand Martins. Details on these birds can be obtained in any good book on ornithology. The following species have also been noted in the area: Mute Swan, on the Inagh Estuary between Liscannor and Lahinch; Duck, on the Corcass behind the 18-Hole Golf Course; Knots can be found on the Inagh Estuary; Oyster Catchers can be seen round the rock pools just south of Lahinch. Goldcrest: Great Tit, Blue Tits, Marsh Tits, Long Tailed Tits, Hedge Sparrow, Mistle Thrush, Song Thrush, Red Wing, Field Fare, Chaffinch, Goldfinch, Linnet, Whinchat, Stonechat, Bullfinch, Greenfinch, Yellow Hammer, Pied Wagtail, Grey Wagtail, Curlew, Rock Dove, Dipper, Wood Pigeon, Moorhen, Cuckoo, Kingfisher, Sparrowhawk, Lapwing, Wren and Kestrel have also been noted. The best viewing areas are the Corcass Inagh Estuary, Lahinch Seafront and rock pools, The Moy River and Woods, Glenville Woods, and for the more common species, Lahinch village.

SEABIRDS NEED THE SEA

All the birds nesting on the cliff below the Tower depend upon the sea for their food. Some feed on the surface of the sea and others, such as the Guillemot, "fly" underwater for fish. In the winter time the cliffs here are usually deserted and silent. Some seabirds go out to sea and do not return to land until the spring.

OIL AT SEA IS A SPECIAL THREAT

Because they spend so much of their lives on the sea, birds like Razorbills, Guillemots and Puffins are easily affected by slicks of oil spills from ships or drilling rigs. If large numbers of birds become oiled and die, few will remain to return to the Cliffs of Moher and breed.

Birds have been counted on the cliffs since 1971. Recent counts have shown an increase in breeding Kittiwakes and Fulmars. Razorbills and Guillemots appear unchanged. Through these counts we shall know if pollution or global warming begins to affect the seabirds in the West of Ireland as it does in other parts of the world. See Table 1 for current bird counts. Table 2 shows bird counts for the early 1970s.

BIRD COUNTING

In order to make counting easier and more accurate, detailed sketch maps are drawn of each colony. Every ledge on which Guillemots breed, and the areas where Kittiwakes and other species nest are given numbers. In June, a series of careful counts are made using binoculars and a telescope.

	PUFFIN	GUILLEMOT	KITTIWAKE	RAZORBILL	FULMAR
GOAT ISLAND (FRONT)	1800	128	61	39	14
O'BRIEN'S TOWER (BENEATH)	500	350	16	27	30
SOUTH PLATFORM (BENEATH)		664	165	11	117
GOAT ISLAND (BACK)	480	610	105	44	71
SEA STACK		2920	271		
TOTAL	2780	4672	618	121	232

summer 2007 | TABLE 1

	GUILLEMOTS	KITTIWAKE	RAZORBILLS
SEA STACK 1974	1,079 birds	257 nests	51 birds
SEA STACK 1975	1,036 birds	257 nests	56 birds

1974/75 | TABLE 2

BOOK 2

THE CLIFFS OF MOHER

HISTORY
MYTH &
LEGEND

EAMONN KELLY B.Ed., Ph.D.

"THE HAG WAS NAMED 'MAL' AND PURSUED CUCHULLIN TO LOOP HEAD, SPRANG AFTER HIM TO DIARMUID AND GRAINNE'S ROCK AND SHE WAS DASHED TO PIECES IN ATTEMPTING TO SPRING BACK AGAIN. HER BLOOD REDDENED THE SEA TO MOHER AND GAVE MALBAY ITS NAME."

- County Clare Folk Tales and Myths – T.J. Westropp

Images clockwise from top left
Entrance to St. Bridget's Well
O'Brien's Coat of Arms
O'Brien's Monument
St. Bridget's Crosses

THE CLIFFS OF MOHER IN HISTORY, MYTH AND LEGEND

The area surrounding the Cliffs of Moher is well chronicled, and its fascinating history is supplemented by legends and stories stretching back into the mists of time. O'Brien's Tower is, perhaps, associated with the locality's more recent history, but it serves as an excellent vantage point from which to see the many other historic landmarks of the region: places steeped in legend, folklore and mythology.

First built in 1835 by Cornelius O'Brien, M.P., the local landlord, O'Brien's Tower consisted of four distinct sections – for more information see page 44 and photo page 66. Before its restoration it had been reduced to two sections, but now it has been renovated and an archway added – Page 68.

A local chronicler, H.B.H., in 1891 described the tower thus: "There is a kitchen for cooking purposes and a spacious room overhead to obtain a view".

Ferguson, writing in 1812, said of the view: "I know of no other spot of equal altitude, where one can look from so dizzy a height down to the sea".

Facing Page:
An aerial view showing O'Brien's Tower, behind it Aill na Shearrach (Cliff of the Foals) and northwards to Doolin and the Burren.
Image courtesy of Shannon Development

HOW THE CLIFFS WERE NAMED

The Cliffs take their name from an old fort that once stood on Hag's Head, the most southern point of the Cliffs, the writer T.J. Westropp refers to it as Moher Ui Ruis or Moher Ui Ruidhin.

The Fort still stood in 1780. The following account is taken from John Lloyd's A Short Tour Of Clare (1780):

"On the western cape or headland lies the famous old fort Ruain, call'd Mohar, which is nearly the same as Fort in the Irish language; this Mohar is the summit of a very high, stupendous cliff surrounded with a stone wall, a part of which is up; inside of it is a green Plain which exhibits a clear Prospect of the gloomy Highlands of Eyr Connaught. The Isles of Aren, of almost the whole coast of Malbay…"

The field where the fort stood is still called "Moher a Thairbh".

The present tower built near the site of the old Moher Ui Ruidhin was built by the British as a lookout tower during the Napoleonic Wars (see Ordnance Map Page 38).

CILL STUIFIN

A disturbed area of water south of Hag's Head and visible on the horizon from Lahinch has been tied to the Atlantis myth. The following early story is adapted from a manuscript entitled *"The adventures of the three sons of Thorailbh Mac Stain"* by Comyn (1750).

"Three brothers, Crochaun, Dahlin and Saul, from the forts bearing their names on Loop Head, were three brothers to whom a druid foretold a fearful end if their beautiful and only sister ceased to be a virgin. Accordingly, they built a fort for her, still called Cathair na hAon Mná – the fort of the lone woman – and three other forts to guard her at Cahercrochaun, Cahersaul and Dundahlin. For long they guarded her, until their cattle were 'driven' or carried away by three other brothers of Corcomroe. These were Ceannuir of Lios Ceannuir, Ruadhan of Moher Ui Ruadhain and Stuithin of Kil Stuithin (Cill Stuifin), an enchanted fort under the sea at Liscannor. Encumbered by the spoils of Corcavaskin the plunderers had only reached its northern end near Lehinch, before the irate owners overtook them. The Corcomroe man had only time to place the cattle on Creachoilean (Island of Plunderers), before O'Brien's Bridge at Dough, before they were fiercely assailed.

The Corcavaskin men prevailed, slaying three chiefs and slaying the majority of their soldiers and destroyed the forts of Moher and Liscannor, but they found the island of Kil Stuithin surrounded by a wall of water and were obliged to leave it unravaged.

They returned in triumph to Loop Head to find their sister, on whose celibacy their lives depended, eloped with Diarmuid Ui Duibhne.

Diarmuid had been promised the hand of the most beautiful woman in Ireland if he won a hurling match being played by the legendary Fianna. Diarmuid won the match and was instructed by Aengus that the most beautiful woman in Ireland lived in Cathair na hAon Mná, Loop Head."

"However, Aengus, also warned of the wrath of the three brothers, and how one of the brothers was the most feared swordsman in Ireland, and a second brother was deadly with the sling. As a safeguard he presented Diarmuid with a magic red ring. The ring had the power of turning green if the brothers were not on Loop Head.

Diarmuid was also told that if he met Piast Dabhran, a mythical monster who lived in Poll a Phiast on the cliffs near Loop Head, the magic ring would deprive the hideous snake-like monster of one third of its strength.

The amorous Diarmuid waited on Mount Brandon until the ring changed slowly from red to green. He then set off across Loop Head in his magic square currach and reached the lady.

She consented gladly to fly with him but as they passed Poll a Phiast a great rumbling was heard. The water boiled and the fearsome Piast raised its hideous head from the water trashing the water madly with its tail.

Diarmuid ripped off the ring and forced it into the monster's mouth. Yet the Piast still had two thirds of its strength and threatened to capsize the little boat.

Just then, Diarmuid's lady love tapped his shoulder and offered the sword and sling she had taken as keepsakes of Loop Head and her brothers. Afire with new hope and using all his skill with sword and sling Diarmuid finally defeated the dreaded Piast Dabhran."

"Three brothers returned to see the couple landing far away in Kerry. They traced her foot prints to Aill a dTruir – the cliff of the three – and fearing a horrible fate if they awaited their doom, they seized each others hands and sprang over the cliffs into the hungry seas."

Cill Stuifin could only be resurrected by the use of a golden key, which was lost when Stiuthin was killed. Westropp records: "The key lies buried with the hero Conan (died 295 A.D.), under his Ogham-inscribed slab on the side of Mount Callan." According to a legend, which still exists, a six-fingered child will be born to a native of the area and this unique child will be able to locate the key. This child will then walk to Clahan, a mile north of Liscannor, and there re-open the gates to Cill Stuifin.

This will cause enormous floods that will destroy Lahinch and Galway. An old Irish poem quoted by a local story-teller, Mr. John Nagle, goes as follows:

"Arann do bhi,
Cill Stuifin ata
Gaillimh a Bheith."

"Aran was (covered by water),
Cill Stuifin is,
Galway will be."

Creachoilean (Island of Plunder).
A view across the Liscannor Bridge and the Inagh River with the ruin of Dough Castle (1422) on the Lahinch Golf Course.

Facing Page:
Shell of Liscannor Castle

And another legend has it that once in seven years Cill Stuifin's golden domes rise over the waves, but with ill omen to anyone who sees them, for the beholder must die before they reappear when seven years have passed by.

A more scientific explanation of Cill Stuifin is given by Westropp: "Cill Stuifin, is actually a dangerous reef at the mouth of Liscannor Bay. In 1839, it was called Kilstuiffin and said to have been an island monastery overwhelmed by an earthquake."

"All our annals record between 799 and 802 show Inis Fitae, on the coast of Corcavaskin, was split into three (the Aran Islands?) by the sea and there was a storm of thunder and lighting on the day before St. Patrick's Day; over a thousand perished, while heaps of sand and rocks were thrown up on the coast. Is it too daring to conjecture that the island and church of Cill Stuifin perished in that great catastrophe, and that its legend, like that of Mutton Island (an island off Milton Malbay) rests on some historic basis?"

HOW HAG'S HEAD WAS NAMED

There are, in fact, two versions – both of which were recorded by T.J. Westropp. The first interpretation says:
"The Hag was named 'Mal' and pursued Cuchullin to Loop Head, sprang after him to Diarmuid and Grainne's Rock (the same Diarmuid and Grainne who feature in the Cill Stuifin legend) and she was dashed to pieces in attempting to spring back again. Her blood reddened the sea to Moher and gave Malbay its name."

On Hag's Head there are two large rock protrusions. That nearer the castle is in the shape of a woman's head, giving rise to the second explanation "the rock has assumed the shape of a seated woman, the Sphynx-like head looking eternally westward to the setting sun."

Facing Page:
A view of Hag's Head from the south showing the Sphynx-like head formation and the ruins of a Napoleonic Lookout Tower.

THE SPANISH ARMADA

At least thirty ships of Philip of Spain's mighty Armada, sent to invade England in the summer of 1588, perished along the coast of Ireland, mainly along the western seaboard. The Armada had been routed by the English in the Channel and off Calais; after its defeat, the fleet sailed up the east coast of England, around the northern tip of Scotland, turning southwards round Ireland for home.

"Implacable I, the old implacable Sea:
Implacable most when most I smile serene –
Pleased, not appeased, by myriad wrecks in me".

- Herman Melville, 1888.

The following authentic account is taken from Westropp's "Ancient Remains near Lehinch, Co. Clare", and is based on the letters of Boetius Clanchy, Sheriff of the area at the time of the Armada.

"It was a wild and stormy day in September (Sep. 5th, 1588), and the light was dying out westward over the great rollers of the Atlantic, when the watchers on the towering cliffs of Moher saw two sails beyond Aran, and in the dim twilight, fancied they saw others farther out to sea."

"They brought the news to Liscannor in the gathering dusk to the Sheriff, Boetius Clanchy. We can imagine the excitement and speculation that buzzed round the numerous watch fires that flickered on the bare walls of Sir Turlough's Castle as the dark, long night passed slowly away.

Another grey day of storm and roaring of the waves had dawned and there in Coolrone (south of Hag's Head) – the seal's creek – the bay to the west of the castle lay a strange vessel.

We can picture to ourselves that hapless waif, the Zuniga, one of the mightiest of the ships of that mightiest of fleets, with her lofty wooden castles, gilt-painted and carved, rising high above the middle deck to stern and bow, her tall, tapering masts (it may be still flying the wind beaten flag of Castile and Leon) and the cross yards – armed with sharp reaping hooks to cut the cordage of the English ships, with which the Spaniards were too slow to grapple or even meet.

The lonely bay, harbour of gulls and seals, was sheltered from the northwest gale, a primary guest that morning. A cock boat, bigger than those of the English vessels, drifted away from the ship, a red anchor was painted conspicuously on its side, it was seen attempting to land, but, even in the bay, the surf ran high, no one got ashore, and only some wreckage and an oil jar landed on the strand inside Liscannor.

Later on in the day, two apparent merchants came ashore and were met and questioned; they were patron and purser of the ship, and implored to be allowed to buy water."

Whether (as in Kilrush) they offered a cask of wine for every one of water are not told, but there, they were so maddened by thirst that they offered a great ship with all its ordnance and furniture to be allowed to take a supply of water.

"Evil was their destiny; as that of the doomed ship of the Ancient Mariner in the snake seething waters of the great calm.

Clanchy's emissary, having got the Spaniards into his power now showed his fangs, and sprang on them. The patron barely escaped in the boat to the galliass – which still lay dangerously near the sands 'out against Dogh I Conor'.

The prisoner was brought to camp – he was one Pedro Baptiste of Naples, and an examination told that the galleass was the 'Zuniga', and that death was busy on board, the master and four men having died since they anchored on the coast.

His fate is not recorded but the history and local tradition show that in the hands of Clanchy and in the jaws of the sea and the pestilence, equal mercy was to be found. The crew of the Zuniga made no other attempt to land."

"… two other ships drifted down the coast, the one to wrecked on the reef between Mutton Island and Tromra, the second at the mouth of the Dunbey creek opposite Dunmore."

MAURA RUA

Maura is simply the Irish for "Mary", Rua is the word for red, so red-haired Mary! She was a warrior chieftainess who lived at the time of the Cromwellian Wars in the mid 17th century and went to some considerable length to hold on to her possessions.

In his ***Co. Clare Folk Tales and Myths (1913)***, Westropp writes: "Maura Rhue – Little Mary – or, by some English speakers, 'Moll Roo', used to hang her maids by their hair from the corbels on the old peel tower (the nucleus of the building). Others said she cut off the breasts of her maids.

I was told in that she married 25 husbands, all the later ones for a year and a day, after which either of the pair could divorce the other.

She was a Mac Mahon and had red hair (whence her name), and she and Conor O'Brien used to ride at the head of their troop in the wars.

General Ireton (a British general besieging Limerick at the time) was attacked by Conor O'Brien, fell mortally wounded but would not surrender. (Lady Chatterton's account of 1839 states: 'Mary captured and hanged the man who wounded Conor.')

His servants brought him back, nearly dead, to Maura at Leme-nagh. She neither sobbed nor wept but shouted to them from the top of the tower: 'What do I want with a dead man here?'. However, on hearing he wasn't dead but was still alive she nursed him tenderly till he died."

"Then she put on a magnificent dress, called her coach, and set off at once to Limerick, which was being besieged by Ireton.
"At the outposts she was stopped by a sentinel, and roared and shouted and cursed at him until Ireton and his officers, who were at dinner, heard the noise and came out. On their asking who she was, she replied –

"I was Conor O'Brien's wife yesterday and his widow today."
"He fought for us yesterday. How can you prove he is dead?"
"I'll marry any of your officers that asks me!"
Captain Cooper, a brave man, at once took her at her word and they were married, so that she saved the O'Brien property for her son, Sir Donat….

"At Lemenagh, it is added that one morning, after her marriage to Cooper, they quarrelled while he was shaving, and he spoke slightingly of Conor O'Brien. The affectionate relict, unable to bear any slur on the one husband she had loved jumped out of bed and gave Cooper a kick in the stomach from which he died."
Another version not quoted by Westropp, of the same incident says that: …'as Maura was jumping out of bed she grabbed a broomstick and hurled it violently at Cooper. The broomstick hit the back of Cooper's head jerking it forward and causing the open razor which Cooper was using to shave with, to cut his throat.'
Westropp continues: "At Carnelly, after killing the last of her 25 husbands, in the year 1673, Maura Rua was taken by her enemies and was fastened up a hollow tree…" and there her story fades out rather ambiguously. Only, the story doesn't end there! Afterwards, her red haired ghost was reputed to haunt the long front avenue near the Druid's altar.

Lemanagh Castle
This was the home of the infamous Maura Rua. Note the small arched brick construction (centre of the picture). This now stands in the garden of Dromoland Castle (see Facing Page:). The gate bears the O'Brien Coat of Arms along with the names of Conor O'Brien and his wife Maura (Rua) Ni Mahon. The inscribed date is 1643. The castle comprises two distinct sections – the old peel tower on the eastern side with slit windows (1480) and the new section on the western side with spacious windows (1640). The gardens of the castle once contained stables and a fish pond.

Facing Page:
Lemanagh Castle arched structure at Dromoland Castle

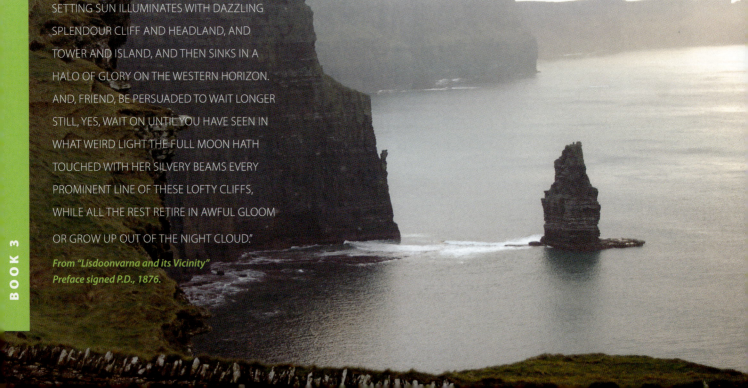

BOOK 3

"VISIT MOHER AGAIN AND STAY ON WHILE THE SETTING SUN ILLUMINATES WITH DAZZLING SPLENDOUR CLIFF AND HEADLAND, AND TOWER AND ISLAND, AND THEN SINKS IN A HALO OF GLORY ON THE WESTERN HORIZON. AND, FRIEND, BE PERSUADED TO WAIT LONGER STILL, YES, WAIT ON UNTIL YOU HAVE SEEN IN WHAT WEIRD LIGHT THE FULL MOON HATH TOUCHED WITH HER SILVERY BEAMS EVERY PROMINENT LINE OF THESE LOFTY CLIFFS, WHILE ALL THE REST RETIRE IN AWFUL GLOOM OR GROW UP OUT OF THE NIGHT CLOUD."

From "Lisdoonvarna and its Vicinity"
Preface signed P.D., 1876.

THE CLIFFS OF MOHER

A GUIDE OF THE LOCALITY

EAMONN KELLY B.Ed., Ph.D.

WALKING TOUR AND RAMBLERS' MAP

To see the majestic Cliffs of Moher at their most impressive, one must travel the area on foot. Driving from viewing point deprives the visitor of much of the grandeur of this rock-bound coast.

O'Brien's Tower is a natural starting point for the walker. From here "the noblest view of the Cliffs can be obtained from a lofty headland" and northwards across Galway Bay, the Connemara coast and the Twelve Bens mountain range can be seen. In Galway Bay itself lie the three Aran Islands – Inisheer, Inishmaan and Inish Mór, immortalized by John Millington Synge and later the location of Robert Flaherty's classic film, "Man of Aran".

Southwards, the coast of Clare comes into view, and further on Mount Brandon and Kerry's Blasket Islands can be seen on clear days. Closer, across Liscannor Bay, rises Slieve Callan (391 m).

At the apex of Liscannor Bay lies Lahinch, framed by its two golf courses; the Inagh River can also be seen, and also the town of Ennistymon.

Liscannor lies on the side of the Bay closest to the Cliffs, a fishing village which was the home of Cornelius O'Brien, who built the tower which still bears his name.

Pre 1900 photograph. Note O'Brien's Tower and An Branán Mór sea stack as they appeared before the turn of the century. Due to the weathering processes, the stack has now lost its needle point.

Turning our attention to the Cliffs themselves, we see to the north a cliff with a broken headland: (1), Aill na Shearrach, "the cliff of the foals". The headland is "Carrig a dTrial" (2) (Cor-ig a dreel), or "the rock of their testing", the origin of the name being unknown. The name possibly derives from "Carraig a Bhraoill" (Cor-ig a vreel) or "the rock of the Cormorants", since these common black sea birds congregate there. It is interesting to note that the sheer rock cliff just north of O'Brien's Tower is also called Aill na Shearrach.

Mr. Brendan Vaughan, a Liscannor school teacher, who studied the Irish placenames of the Cliffs, has provided the following interpretation of Aill na Shearrach. 'In pre-Christian Ireland, in the time of the legendary Tuatha de Danaan, sorcery and druidism held sway. After St. Patrick, however, the old rituals were gradually abandoned. In protest, the Tuatha de Danaan employed their magical powers to change themselves into horses, and galloped to Kilcornan, there to hide for centuries in the Kilcornan caves. Down the years the horses were forgotten until one day seven glistening white foals emerged from the caves into the bright daylight for the first time in countless years. Startled and frightened, the foals bolted, and galloped madly to Aill na Shearrach, there to meet their fate.'

Previous Page:
An Branán Mór sea stack 200 feet high approximately.

A view of the Tower from Aill na Shearrach itself gives an idea of the huge numbers and variety of the sea birds which nest on the cliff edges.

3 To the north of O'Brien's Tower lies Slieve na Giorrai, "the mountain of the hares".

4 The large sea stack is known as An Branán Mór; the origin of the name is uncertain, though it may be derived from Brendan, as is Mount Brandon, for example **5** O'Brien's Tower itself is discussed later.

6 Goat Island is, in fact, a promontory, so named because Cornelius O'Brien kept goats there, lowering them from the Cliffs by ropes. A puck goat, apparently, being made available at mating time! The "island" has some magnificent stacks of rock, and holds a large puffin colony.

7 The sandstone ledge below the main viewing platform rises approximately 152m sheer from sea level.

8 Leach Maire na Gniomh – "The Flagstone of Mary of the Deeds", refers to the infamous Maire Rua, whose life story is discussed in Book II, History, Myth & Legend.

9 The Stuaicin Cliff. In Irish, "stuaic" refers to apex, and this is thought to be the highest point of the Cliffs – 179 m.

10 Aill na hEan – "The Cliffs of the Birds".

11 Breanan Beag - the smaller version of An Branán Mór.

12 Aill na hUan - "the cliff of the lambs". According to the story, one early spring a number of the ewes rambled along a path near here; their rescuers succeeded in getting them to safety, but had to contend with two newly-born lambs with every ewe!

13 Poll na hUisce – "The Water Hole". Named after the fresh water well which is found here.

14 Cruis – "Quarry." So called because of the renowned Liscannor flagstones are mined here. Another quarry lies some distance from the Cliffs opposite Breanan Beag, while the principal quarry is located further north in Luogh.

15 Between Cruis and the Natural (or Sea) Arch are two fairly small caves.

16 The Natural Arch itself is best viewed from Hag's Head.

17 The origin of Meall Mór and Meall Beag is uncertain, but the word meall is usually taken to mean a narrow stretch of land.

18 Ronseach – "a rough, rocky area".

19 Maide Sníomh – "a wooden needle", used for net mending. The "needle eye" refers to a sea arch.

20 Cathaoir – "a chair"; this refers to the Sea Stump, discussed on Page 47.

21 Ceann Toll – "Ceann" is headland, and the origin of "Toll" is uncertain.

22 Bullan Donall – "Donal's Bull" – origin unknown.

Aill na Shearrach

23 Leach a dTri Licin – "the flagstones of three rivulets" (or wells).

24 Hag's Head – the origin of the name is discussed in Book II.

From Hag's Head, looking north, is one of the most beautiful, though neglected, views of the Cliffs of Moher.

The cliffs south of Hag's Head afford an unforgettable prospect, including a spectacular sea arch at its tip. Writing in 1780, John Lloyd said: "This wonderful promontory, almost encompassed by devouring seas, and the opposite wild coast, really affords a horrible and tremendous aspect vastly more to be dreaded than accounted". And in 1835, the following was Ferguson's view: "The rock is more argillaceous than on the southern portion of the field, and especially when lighted by the rays of the evening sun, is full of colour. Seen from the ocean at sunset, the range of the Cliffs looks, in truth, like a mighty wall of brass". Hag's Head rises to a height of 122 m above sea level.

25 Poll Caum. This is a serpentine gorge which is worth seeing. The name means "Narrow hole or inlet".

26 The large hill behind Poll Caum is known as Cnoc an Iolar – the hill of the eagle", a name which may refer to peregrine falcons.

27 Aill a Chaoirigh – "the cliff of the sheep". No known explanation

28 Collun na Geige – "the column of the geese". Origin Unknown

29 Cuinne Mór – "the great corner".

30 Poll Gorm – "the blue hole".

31 Carraig Mhaire Chiuin – "the rock of quiet Mary". Origin unknown.

32 Loch na Saggart – "the pool of the priests". According to the story, during the English persecution of the Catholics in the time of the Penal Laws (18th century), two priests were fleeing from their captors towards the cliffs. They were captured, executed, and their bodies thrown over the cliffs. Immediately, so the story goes, a fresh water well sprung up at this spot.

PROMONTORIES – NOS. 1 & 6

When cliffs are composed of different types of rock they are eroded unequally. The resultant structure is a headland or promontory.

A magnificent example of a promontory can be seen below O'Brien's Tower – Goat Island.

A second example is seen at the end of Aill na Shearrach; north of O'Brien's tower.

Most of the eroded material from the cliffs is carried to sheltered coves and forms shingle beaches (i.e. at the promontory of Aill na Shearrach, Page 43). Examples of these beaches can be seen looking northwards from Hag's Head.
Much of the finer rock and sand is carried further north to Doolin Strand.

Facing Page:
Goat Island

O'Brien's Tower

SEA CAVE – NO. 15 (ON PRIOR MAP)

The sea cliffs facing you have been formed by the continuous process of sea erosion. Tons of sea water are hurled at the cliff base, pounding, crushing and weakening the rock structures which are then wrenched away out to sea.

Air is also trapped and compressed against the cliff face, forced into rock crevices, and, when allowed to expand further weakens the battered stone. As this process advances a sea cave is formed. An enormous sea cave faces you as you look towards the south. For other caves on the cliffs, see the Ordnance Map on the inside front cover.

SEA ARCH – NO. 16

When two sea caves at opposite ends of a headland meet, a sea arch is formed.
A sea arch can be viewed from O'Brien's Tower with binoculars. It is situated at the bottom of the cliff as on the map.
A better view of this sea arch can be had from Hag's Head. A second marvellous sea arch can also be seen at the tip of Hag's Head if viewed from south of Hag's Head promontory.
In Irish, this sea arch is known as "Maide Sniomh" because it resembles the large wooden needles used for mending fishing nets.

SEA STACK – NOS. 4 & 11

"…the abrupt and towering ramparts of flagstones and shale, the rock pinnacles, whirling gulls and choughs and the long curves of the dazzling foam far below."

The sea arch is now, in turn, placed under siege by the relentless sea until finally the uppermost section of the arch collapses. A sea stack is now formed.

Two examples of sea stacks can be seen off the cliffs. The first is visible as you look towards Hag's Head; the second is situated below O'Brien's Tower.

The Irish word "Breanan" is thought to refer to a monument or pillar. "Mór" and "beag" mean "big" and "small" respectively. The An Branán Mór is about 200 ft high (No. 4)

SEA STUMP – NO. 20

The sea arch is now subjected to weathering processes and continued sea erosion. It is finally reduced to a sea stump which will eventually be covered by the sea.

Two sea stumps are visible from the Cliffs (one at Hag's Head) at low tide. At full tide, they are seen as disturbed areas on the blue carpets of the sea as the "breaking surge and sheeted foam" (Westropp) wash over them.

A SHORT TOUR OF LAHINCH, LISCANNOR AND OTHER AREAS

Lahinch caters well for holiday-makers. Writing in 1891, H.B.H. in his "Holiday Haunts of the West Coast of Clare", said: "its strand for length, width and evenness is not to be excelled in Ireland. The accommodation is excellent, neat and respectable, and so graduated in size and arrangement as to admit of being let at prices to suit the position and circumstances of all classes."

What more can we say, today, except that the town's facilities are ultra modern with two excellent golf courses (one of them a championship links) as well as the Lahinch Seaworld which houses an indoor swimming pool, cafeteria, aquarium and gym. Other amenities include a fun fair, surfing and fishing facilities.

Lahinch is bounded to the south by the Moy River, to the north by the Inagh River, and to the West by the Atlantic. In effect, it is a peninsula, or half island, which was in fact, the old Irish name for the town – Leath Inis. However, the official Irish name for the town is An Leacht/Leacht Ui Chonchuir. Leacht means a commemorative mound of stones, and probably refers to the grave of O'Connor of Corcomroe – "who was slain by his nephew, Donnchadh, in 1741." The site of his grave is said to be located beneath "The Spinnaker" public house in Lahinch.

Lahinch

Pre 1900 photograph. The sloping promenade (centre of picture) was washed away in 1878. This sea wall, which cost the county nearly £4,000 at the time was washed away by the late Spring Tide with considerable damage to the lodges in front of the beach. The problem was due to a sandy foundation. History, it seems, repeated itself. Most of the new car park was washed away after nearly one hundred years. Are these two minor disasters forerunners of a major catastrophe (See "Cill Stuifin" Page 26). A new sloped promenade has been added to the rough area (right foreground of the picture). The narrow strip of land between the river and the house tops represents the 18 hole golf course. Note the sandy area (left background of the picture) which was owned by a family called Parkinson who sold sand for building and gardening purposes at one shilling (at the time) a cart load.

Liscannor

Pre 1900 photograph. Note the three horse drawn carts and the collection of famous Moher flagstones which were quarried at the Cliffs of Moher. Of interest also are the clothes of the gentlemen and the fashion of the child standing barefoot in front of the Temperance Bar (Blake's Antiques in the 1970s, currently the Cliffs of Moher Hotel).

Along the cliffs south of Lahinch to Cregg beach is a lovely walk where there is a curiously configurated hillside covered with gorse and cut into three sections by deep trenches. This is Doon Maeve – the fort of Maeve – and a century ago, Westropp offered the following advice to archaeologists:

"A certain man began to dig up the space inside its trenches. Before he had been long at work he fell down and lay to all appearances dead. News was brought at once to a reputed "wise woman" who was evidently equal to the emergency. She rushed to the nearest fairy fort, performed some magic, and ran to Doon Maeve to her apparently lifeless husband. She addressed herself to the unseen inhabitants of the fort and imperiously ordered them to bring back her husband at once. Immediately, the insensible man sat up and recovered complete strength while a stick was carried off his stead".

On the newer 18 hole golf course stands an old ruined castle. This Westropp records, was called Dough Castle, and was built by Donncadh, son of Donal O'Conor, in 1422. Its present day ruin is just one of the many links with Ireland's historic and stormy history to be seen in the area.

Discussing Lahinch and its environs in 1887, the "Dublin Journal" somewhat prophetically summed it all up - "The district will assuredly advance by leaps and bounds to be one of the prettiest and most popular resorts in Ireland".

GARLAND SUNDAY

Traditionally held on the last Sunday in July, "Garland Sunday" is an annual festival staged in many parts of Munster which was well described and documented by Kathleen Knox, writing in "The Irish Monthly" back in 1894. She said: "On that day as many as from three to four thousand visitors find their way to Lahinch from Ennis, Corofin, Ennistymon, Miltown Malbay and even greater distances…"

"Among the thronging crowds there are probably a few who know or care of the origin of the term "Garland", indeed, so little is understood that the gracefully expressive word is often mispronounced "Garlic" and under its disagreeable metamorphosis commands unbounded popularity. Still, the quaint name may be of interest to those who like to know something of the old customs of the country. In tracing it, we are led back to very primitive days, and a curious light is shed on the poverty and trials with which the people had to contend.

"In Clare, as in other parts of the country, the potato formed the staple food of the poorest class of the peasantry. From the end of April, the supply began to fail, the oatmeal ran out and the fishing could not be depended upon. So with brave hearts the people locked their doors and wandered off to Galway and Roscommon, where they begged a few handfuls of meal until the last week in July. Then they returned home to dig their 'black bulls', the earliest variety of potato known to them. At Lahinch a little festival was made. The men cut down an oak tree – the Irish for Garland Sunday was Donnic cron dhu, which translated means 'The Sunday of the Oak Tree'. The boys and girls decorated it with bits of bright coloured ribbon or cotton and sang and danced around it all day long, as a thanksgiving for the much-needed fruits of the earth; and it is the lingering shadow of this old custom which still draws the people together".

LISCANNOR

The original Irish name for this district was Tuatha Reanna – "The headland country" – but the title Lios Ceannuir appears in the State Paper for 1601. Loosely translated, the name means "The Headland Fort of the Massacre", though no record of a massacre survives.

However, Frost's "Place Names of County Clare" (1906) claimed that Ceannuir derived from Conchubair, meaning "Connor", a family of which name owned the barony of Corcomroe, Page 27.

A fishing village, Liscannor is also renowned for its flagstones, which were exported in olden days. The town's biggest day in recent years was in July 1977, when Admiral Wiggley of the U.S. Navy presented a commemorative tombstone honouring the birthplace of John P. Holland, the inventor of the submarine. The street where the inventor was born and lived for many years has been re-named Holland Street in his memory.

KILMACREEHY

The little churchyard of Kilmacreehy lies between Liscannor and Lahinch, and is named after St. Macreehy who lived there circa 540 A.D. Today it is a "melancholy little place, a long storm-lashed ruin of thin flagstones" (Westropp). Macreehy's Bed is the name which has been given to a flat rock which is visible from the graveyard at low tide; here, tradition has it, the saint did penance.

Above: Lahinch 1842, map courtesy of Clare Library. *Below:* Kilmacreehy Churchyard, 2009

Above: Liscannor 1842. *Below:* Cliffs of Moher 1842, maps courtesy of Clare Library.

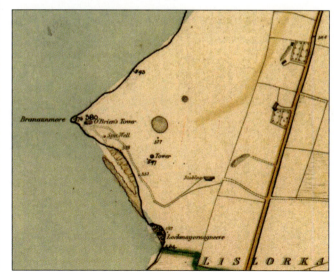

THE CLIFFS OF MOHER

CORNELIUS O'BRIEN M.P.

EAMONN KELLY B.Ed., Ph.D.

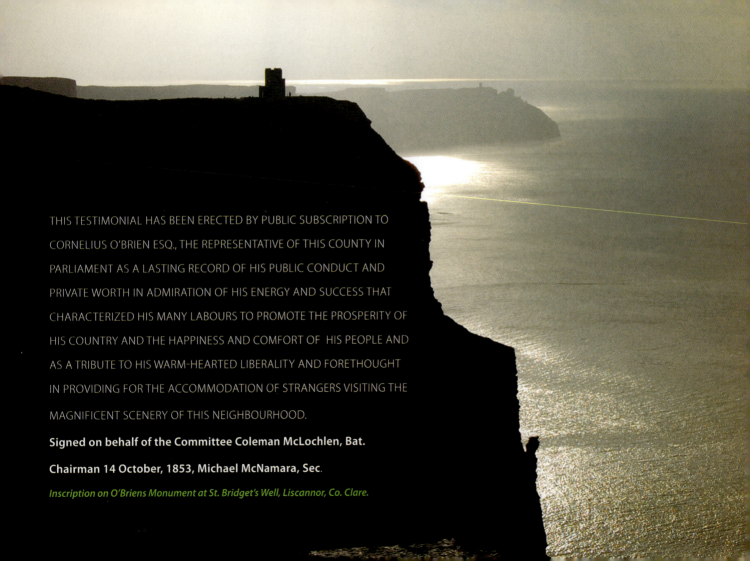

THIS TESTIMONIAL HAS BEEN ERECTED BY PUBLIC SUBSCRIPTION TO CORNELIUS O'BRIEN ESQ., THE REPRESENTATIVE OF THIS COUNTY IN PARLIAMENT AS A LASTING RECORD OF HIS PUBLIC CONDUCT AND PRIVATE WORTH IN ADMIRATION OF HIS ENERGY AND SUCCESS THAT CHARACTERIZED HIS MANY LABOURS TO PROMOTE THE PROSPERITY OF HIS COUNTRY AND THE HAPPINESS AND COMFORT OF HIS PEOPLE AND AS A TRIBUTE TO HIS WARM-HEARTED LIBERALITY AND FORETHOUGHT IN PROVIDING FOR THE ACCOMMODATION OF STRANGERS VISITING THE MAGNIFICENT SCENERY OF THIS NEIGHBOURHOOD.

Signed on behalf of the Committee Coleman McLochlen, Bat.

Chairman 14 October, 1853, Michael McNamara, Sec.

Inscription on O'Briens Monument at St. Bridget's Well, Liscannor, Co. Clare.

Images clockwise from top left
Lawrence Collection images of
Cliffs of Moher from Aill na Shearrach
Liscannor Castle
St. Bridget's Well
Liscannor

Mount Callan in the distance with Liscannor flag fence

CORNELIUS O'BRIEN, M.P.

Cornelius O'Brien, M.P., was a local landlord, who has had a profound effect on the history of the area. His life is well chronicled; today he is still commemorated in O'Brien's Tower, the vantage point of the Cliffs of Moher.

In *The Handbook to Lisdoonvarna,* 1876, the writer stated: "It must be remembered that the Tower, the flag fences, the series of steps, the round table and the coach house, have all been erected at the expense of Cornelius O'Brien, Esq., M.P."

However, the Handbook does scant justice to O'Brien who also had built St. Bridget's Well, the O'Brien Monument, O'Brien's Bridge, O'Brien's Ship, "the Reliever's Well," his own residence, Birchfield House, and the bridge over the Inagh Estuary between Lahinch and Liscannor which was completed in 1836.

The Flag Fences, mentioned above, can be seen running the entire length of the cliffs. They are the result of a bet made by O'Brien with another landlord that he would be able to build a wall "six feet high and one inch thick" over a given distance. Using the local Liscannor flags, he won easily.

But O'Brien became involved with Liscannor flags for other reasons: he decided to build a ship to transport them to lucrative markets in England.

The ship was built outside the Grand Gate of his mansion, Birchfield House. When completed, he arranged for the ship to be moved on wooden rollers to the quay, half a mile away.

Facing Page: *Hag's Head and Watch Tower*

Liscannor Harbour

This is a most interesting and historical photograph as it shows the loading of Moher Flag as it looked at the time of Cornelius O'Brien. Note also the steam driven engine which has pushed two large trailers onto the pier. In the foreground can be seen tar and canvas boats called currachs. A barrel raft can be seen in the left foreground.

Facing Page:

This picture offers a rare glimpse of the Round Table built by O'Brien (now removed). Note the old style hat of the seated gentleman, the two stout bottles on the table and the barefoot child seated on the platform. Note also the cave, the Breanan Beag and sea stack and Hag's Head in the distance. For scale, notice the person on the top edge of the nearest cliff.

"A parish of men" (to use a local phrase) was needed to shift it, and the whole operation took three days of toil and sweat. When the ship was launched it was loaded with its cargo of flags and set sail.

Loading of the cargo of flags involved a definite ritual. The flags were pulled by a one-horse cart from the quarry to the weighing yard (Tynes). The entire cart and load were weighed and the weight of the cart (usually 6 cwt.) was subtracted. The flags alone had to weigh one ton, and the rate of exchange was "two bob a ton" at the time.

The entire operation, "dressing the stone" at the quarry, ferrying it to the quay, and loading it on the ship earned the workman "eight and sixpence". The rent was £17 a year.

But O'Brien's ship was soon in trouble. "It never dried all day she sailed, rain, teeming rain". A strong wind sprung up off Kerry Head, and forced her ashore. She could not be steered from danger, because the teeming rain had swollen the new ropes in their pulleys, and no response came from the sails. The rough Kerry coast ravaged the ship and its cargo of toil and sweat was lost.

To accommodate tourists, O'Brien had a round table built on the large cliff ledge beneath the viewing platform. People held picnics at the table and history records that Irish dances were also held on the platform. The coach house was located in front of the entrance to the new visitor centre building and for a while during the 1970s and 80s it served as a visitor centre.

CLIFFS OF MOHER. Co. CLARE. 6220. W.L.

St. Bridget's Well

Birchfield House, O'Brien's home, was a castellated structure which can still be seen north of Liscannor. Today, it stands in ruins, surrounding a private farmhouse.

The downfall of the house is said to have been foretold by a priest. The local priest at the time made a deal with O'Brien that he could buy out his land and so would no longer be subject to rent tax. Reconsidering the deal, O'Brien realized that many other tenants would follow suit and tried to revoke the agreement he had made with the priest.

A heated argument arose when O'Brien met the priest. In protest, O'Brien stopped going to Mass, which was not to the priest's liking, since O'Brien was the most influential man in the district. During Mass the priest is reputed to have foretold:

"…that the crows would fly through Birchfield", and that "…within a hundred years, there wouldn't be a tree to be seen in Birchfield".

Facing Page:
St. Bridget's Well

Today, the house is in ruins, and every tree in the estate is dead. But there were other sides to O'Brien's character. A holy well dedicated to St. Bridget delivered him from an illness, and in gratitude he had the well removed from its original location to its present position at the cross roads. O'Brien was also buried at the well. His tomb with its iron grating door, and the O'Brien crest above the entrance can be seen today.

Of St. Bridget's Well, the Dublin Journal 1887 recorded – "On St. Bridget's Day, thousands from all parts of the country make a pilgrimage and fervently pray together, making "round after round with pious intent". An eel is said to live in the well and it is considered a lucky omen to see it.

Across the road from the well is O'Brien's Monument. This was said to have been erected by tenants to testify to O'Brien's kindness, but there are counter-claims that tenants who refused to subscribe risked reprimand and possible eviction.

The O'Brien Coat of Arms appears above the doorway of the Mausoleum on the Reliever's Well (Page 64) and on Dromoland Castle Hotel.

Facing Page:
O'Brien's Tomb

O'Brien's Monument

RELIEVER'S WELL

The Reliever's Well was built by O'Brien on October 14th, 1853 as a source of water for a family known as the Reliever's because they provided relief work for starving peasantry during the Famine. The well is located past O'Brien's Monument, past the farmhouse on the left, as the road from Liscannor curves towards the Cliffs of Moher.

On this well the weather beaten remnants of the O'Brien crest can be seen. This crest was copied and is now part of the archway leading to O'Brien's Tower. Another version of the crest can be seen above the Tomb of O'Brien. The O'Brien motto read "An lamh laidir lamh in Uachtar" - The strong hand, the upper hand.

Reliever's Well

Birchfield House with Liscannor Castle in the distance, early 1900s above, 2009 below

O'BRIEN AND THE DOG LICENCE

One warm lazy afternoon, Cornelius O'Brien, M.P., was driving through the township of Liscannor in his regal coach, proud as the proverbial peacock and feeling "lord of all he surveyed". Just then a little mongrel pup darted between the legs of the horses, snapping at them furiously. The horses bolted, the coach careened wildly across the road and ended up in an undignified heap in the ditch.

Recovering what was left of his composure and trying desperately to look dignified, while knee-deep in swamp-water, O'Brien ordered the owner of "that horrible little beast" to step forward. Nobody moved. The faces of the large crowd of locals who had gathered to watch and wonder, portrayed much amusement.

Purple with indignation and furious that he could prove nothing, O'Brien decreed that herewith and hereinafter any peasant without a licence for his dog would be in dire danger indeed. Having once again asserted his authority and his superiority he plod and squelched his way back to Birchfield House

Facing Page:

A truly unique picture of the Cliffs of Moher showing the original O'Brien's Tower in all its glory. Note the group of people seated at the Round Table on the ledge below the viewing platform. The two sections on the right of the Tower and the Round Table are now just a memory. Note also the flag fences on the cliff edge.

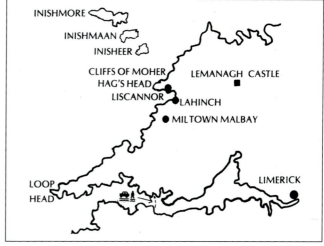

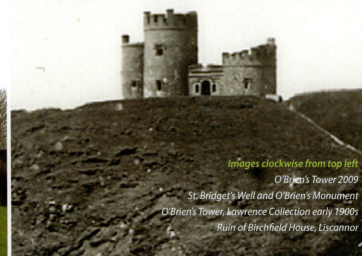

Images clockwise from top left
O'Brien's Tower 2009
St. Bridget's Well and O'Brien's Monument
O'Brien's Tower, Lawrence Collection early 1900s
Ruin of Birchfield House, Liscannor